ALLEN PHOTOGR

CW00891154

TOWING HORSE TRAILERS

CONTENTS

Those who tow horse trailers without finding out what it involves are risking their safety and that of their horses and other road users. You must always put safety and your horses' well-being first.

BUYING A TRAILER

A trailer must be suitable for your horses and your towcar. Small breeds need lowered breast bars and tie-up rings while large horses need good headroom and a trailer able to take their weight.

Weight is the most important consideration when choosing a trailer or towcar. The unladen weight of the trailer, plus the weight of your heaviest horses should not exceed the trailer's maximum authorized mass (gross or maximum laden weight) or the car's maximum towing weight, or the outfit could be dangerous. You may also void the trailer's and car's warranties and risk prosecution.

Ideally, the trailer's laden weight should not exceed 85 per cent of the car's unladen, or kerb, weight, though this can be difficult with larger horses. The closer you get to the car's weight, the more carefully you must tow and

once it weighs more than the car, the tail can wag the dog!

The other important weight is the trailer's noseweight, which is the downward pressure the laden trailer exerts on the towball. You must rely on the trailer manufacturer's estimate because it is impossible to check this with horses aboard. If the noseweight is too high, the car's rear suspension could be too squashed to work properly, while its nose rises to make steering light and stability poor. Too high a towball has the same effect – most trailers require one about 46 cm (18 in) above level ground.

HOW HEAVY IS YOUR HORSE?

You can estimate a horse's weight with a weigh tape, which is used like a tape measure, or by using the following calculation, where the horse's length is measured from the withers to where the tail joins the body.

(Girth in cm, squared x length in cm) divided by 8717 = weight in kg.

PRACTICALITIES

Examine your intended trailer. How steep and wide are the ramps? Can you manage ramps and partitions (alone if necessary)? What fittings are standard? Is it well made and well finished?

A groom's door means that you can get to the horses safely without risk of them getting out on the road.

Galvanizing makes the chassis and body frame last longer and sealed-for-life wheel bearings save maintenance.

SECOND-HAND

If you buy a second-hand trailer from a dealer you have more protection in law, but should still take care. Examine the trailer for signs of damage and neglect. In particular, inspect the floor from above and below for rot, lifting matting and poking any suspect areas with a screwdriver. Aluminium floors should last better than wood but must be examined for damage and corrosion.

Connect up the electrical system to check the lights and, if you can test tow it, feel the wheel centres afterwards for excessive heat from seized bearings or brakes.

Trailers without manufacturers' chassis plates, with signs of chassis marks having been removed or for which paperwork is 'lost', are almost certainly stolen. Some trailer manufacturers keep registers of owners and stolen trailers, so phone them with the chassis

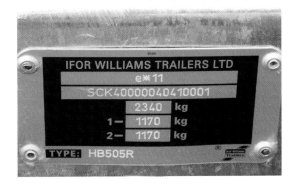

number before buying. Trailers registered with The National Plant and Equipment Register bear a 'TER' sticker and can be checked for a fee, either by calling the number on the sticker or at www.ter-europe.org.

CHOOSING A TOWCAR

Do your homework because few car sales people are horse trailer towing experts, but if they advise against a model, believe them because they get nothing for putting you off!

The technical specification can help you choose likely towcars. Engine performance is shown as power and torque. Power, usually expressed as horsepower (bhp or continental PS), is like the power you see in a racehorse flat out. Torque, the engine's 'twisting power', usually expressed as pounds-feet (lb ft) or Newton metres (Nm), is more akin to a heavy horse getting a big cart moving.

Torque is important for towing. A car with a 'good torque spread' starts developing usable torque at low engine speeds and continues to deliver a useful amount over a wide rev range, giving good flexibility at all speeds and making a good towcar.

When you test drive a potential towcar, if you have to change gear continually without a trailer, it will become hard work when towing. Big gaps between the gear ratios which make, say, third too busy and fourth too high, feel bigger with a trailer. Automatics should change down willingly under power, but not be so over-sensitive that they 'hunt' between gears, which

is rare in modern electronically controlled gearboxes.

Anti-lock brakes (ABS) significantly reduce emergency stopping distances when towing, while electronic traction and stability controls also increase safety margins.

Cars registered after 1 August 1998 can only be fitted with an EC type approved towbar, which bears a label carrying an approval E-number (see photo).

If you buy a second-hand car with a towbar fitted, check that it can take the weight of your trailer and examine the points at which it is attached to the car for damage.

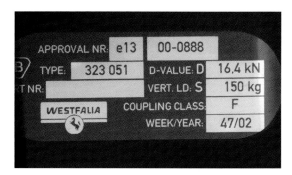

THE LAW

LICENCES

You must hold a full driving licence to tow anything. Most drivers who passed their test before 1 January 1997 have licence categories allowing them to drive vehicle and trailer combinations weighing up to 8.25 tonnes. All the weights quoted here are maximum authorized mass (MAM) unless otherwise stated.

Those passing since 1 January 1997 are allowed to drive a 3.5 tonne vehicle plus a 750 kg trailer. They may also drive a car of under 3.5 tonnes plus a larger braked trailer provided the combination does not exceed 3.5 tonnes and the trailer's MAM is less than the unladen weight of the towcar, whether or not the trailer is laden at the time.

Most horse trailers have a MAM of over 2 tonnes, which is heavier than most cars, so anyone who passed their test after 1 January 1997 has to take a further towing test – officially the B+E test after the licence categories for a car and trailer. New drivers may tow if showing L-plates and accompanied by someone over 21 who has held the B+E licence class for three years, including pre-1997 drivers.

However, for a vehicle with more than eight seats, including some Land Rover Defender 110 Stationwagons, post-1997 drivers must have two years driving experience and take a

minibus test in order to drive it solo, plus a minibus towing test to tow any trailer over 750 kg. Even then, they are limited to trailers with a MAM less than the unladen weight of the minibus.

The tests follow the lorry test, with reversing and braking exercises at lorry test centres. Test details and application forms are available from Driving Standards Agency regional offices or at www.direct.gov.uk. See Guide 44 in this series, *Preparing for the Towing Test*.

Courses Many lorry driving schools run towing test courses, and the British Horse Society website at www.bhs.org.uk has a list under 'training'. The Caravan Club (01342 336808; www.caravanclub.co.uk) and Camping and Caravan Club (0845 1307632; www.campingandcaravanningclub.co.uk) do basic manoeuvring courses and list B+E trainers.

IF IN DOUBT

If you are unsure of what your licence entitles you to drive, ring the Driver and Vehicle Licensing Agency's driver enquiry unit on 0870 240 0009 or visit www.direct.gov.uk.

INSURANCE

Most car insurance includes the legal minimum third party cover for a trailer when it is being towed, but this does not cover damage to or theft of your trailer. Either get an extension to the car policy or take out a separate trailer policy.

TYRES

Car and trailer tyres must have at least 1.6 mm of tread over the central 75 per cent of their width for their entire circumference, though a tyre with under 3 mm offers little grip in the wet. Tyres must be free from deep cuts and bulges (which indicate that they are breaking up) and it is illegal to use cross-ply and radial tyres on the same axle. They must have the correct weight rating for your trailer.

LIGHTS

Trailers must have on the back two red sidelights, two red stop lamps, at least one red fog lamp, an illuminated number plate and two triangular red reflectors, plus amber indicators flashing between 60 and 120 times a minute. They must also show a white sidelight to the front and, if over a certain length, have amber side reflectors.

The regulations state limits on bulb wattages, sizes of reflectors and the maximum and minimum distances between different lights and from lamps to the ground and the trailer sides, so check before making alterations.

HORSE SENSE

There are many livestock transport regulations plus special rules for horses. You are required by law to carry each horse's passport. Vehicles used for equines must have 'adequate' headroom and the EU has considered further headroom requirements for long journeys. When transporting more than one equine you must separate them with a partition unless they are a mare and foal. You must also have a breast bar so the animals can brace against braking.

The floor and ramp must provide reasonable grip, with no more than a 20 cm (8 in) step between them. At night you must have a light to inspect the animals.

Regulations for professional transporters are outside this book's scope, but take care you do nothing that can be interpreted as transporting horses for 'hire or reward', like accepting money from a friend for moving their horse. A groom whose job includes taking horses to shows may need a Welfare of Animals in Transport certificate of competence (see www.defra.gov.uk).

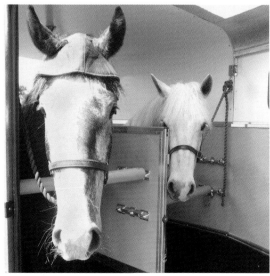

DANGER! It is illegal and dangerous for a person to travel in a trailer.

TRAILER PARTS

1. Towbar
2. Towball
3. Towhitch
4. Hitch locking handle
5. Handbrake
6. Overrun mechanism
7. Breakaway cable
8. Electrical socket
9. Electrical plug
10. Jockey wheel handle
11. Rear ramp
12. Front ramp
13. Groom's door
14. Ramp counterbalance
    spring
15. Side reflector
16. Upper doors
17. Galvanized chassis

18. Rear reflector
19. Breeching bar
20. Partition
21. Breast bar
22. Tie-up ring
23. Interior light
24. Ventilator
25. Slip-resistant flooring

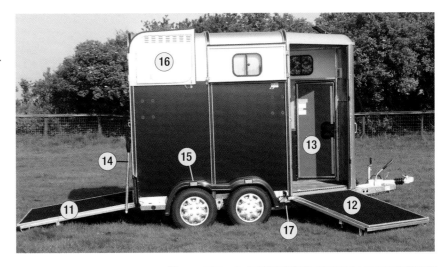

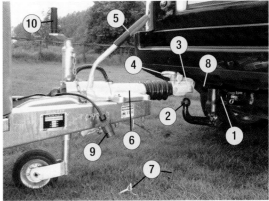

HITCHING UP

Be methodical about hitching and unhitching to avoid omissions. If your towcar's mirrors don't give a good view past the trailer, fit towing mirrors (left). Equibrand's Coupling Mirror (right) allows you to see hitch and ball coming together and can be used for the towing test.

1. Check car and trailer tyre pressures before every trip. If the car manufacturer gives different pressures for different loads, use the fully laden one for towing. If not, some cars tow better with rear pressures about 3 psi higher than normal, but do not exceed the maximum shown on the tyre.

2. Apply the trailer handbrake, remove security devices then wind the jockey wheel to the required height. Check that the towball is greased.

3. Line the centre of the car up with the hitch and reverse slowly – a marker on the rear screen helps. A helper should indicate if you are off line. Place a broom against the hitch if you are alone.

4. Over the last foot or so, your helper uses their hands to show the distance between towball and hitch. (You can't have help on the towing test.)

5. If you stop a little short, judge how far back you are going by comparing the front wheel's movement to something on the ground.

6. Wind the jockey wheel back to lower the hitch onto the towball. Some hitch locking handles must be held up while others automatically latch on.

7. Once the hitch appears locked on, lower the jockey wheel a few turns to lift the back of the vehicle to prove that the hitch is on properly.

8. Fully raise the wheel and lock it securely.

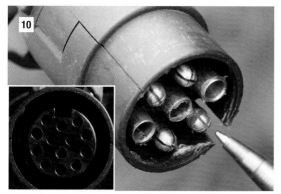

9. Clip the breakaway cable onto the special towbar rings or loop it around the bar or towball neck, making sure it cannot foul the hitch.

⚠ **DANGER! This cable pulls on the trailer brakes if it becomes unhitched so it must not be attached to car parts which may break first.**

10. The electrical plug only fits one way, so line its cut-out up with the lug on the socket. Some cars have two sockets: use the one with the black cover flap because the white flapped one is for charging caravan batteries. A European 13-pin socket (see inset) does both and requires a matching plug or adaptor.

11. Check that cables have enough slack for cornering but will not touch the ground.

12. Check the car's handbrake is on and release the trailer handbrake.

13. Check that lights and indicators are working – car and trailer indicators not matching is a common fault – then get someone to see if the trailer brake lights work.

UNHITCHING

Apply the car and trailer handbrakes before you unhitch. Disconnect and stow the cables. You have to hold the hitch's locking handle up as you wind the jockey wheel down. Always store a trailer with the road wheels chocked and the handbrake off, or the brake shoes will stick to the drums.

HORSE TRAVELLING WEAR

Youngstock may travel without some of the protective clothing because the worry caused by their unfamiliarity presents a greater risk.

Comfort Equestrian's Transit rug (**1**) is useful for youngsters with its padded body and tail protection. It is worn here with a poll guard to protect the head. Leather headcollars (**2**) are safest because they should break before the horse's neck if they get caught up. Boots or bandages (**3**) protect the legs. Bandages must always be used over padding (**4**) for proper protection. A rug (**5**) stops muscles getting chilled but must fit well so there is no risk of it slipping. Rugs should match the state of the horse and the climate, so take spares if necessary. A tailguard (**6**) or tail bandage (**7**) is essential, especially on large horses, to stop them rubbing the skin from their tails.

Carry a bridle to put on over the headcollar for more control during loading and unloading, but never travel a horse in one because terrible injuries can result from bit rings getting caught up.

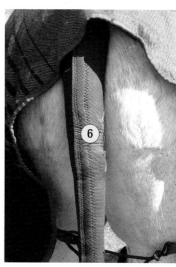

LOADING

The lighter and more inviting you make the trailer, the better. If you have a front ramp, lower it so that the horse can see through the vehicle.

Loading is easier and safer if the central partition is moved over to make the entrance wider. Load the heavier of two horses, or a single horse, on the driver's side to help counter the road's camber. Single horses often travel better with full-width bars and no partition, but should be cross-tied to prevent turning.

Lead the horse walking alongside his head, or slightly in front. Horses often pause as they put their first foot on the ramp, as if checking it, and should be encouraged forwards. Do not look round at the horse if he halts, because he may see this as a reprimand.

If you have a helper, get them to put the breeching bar in place and then raise the ramp while you reassure the horse. They should talk to the horse so he knows they are there.

Always stand to one side while raising the ramp so that if the horse kicks, it is less likely to hit you. Leave the upper rear doors open except in poor weather when spray would be sucked onto the horses. It is unwise to leave front upper doors open.

PROBLEM LOADERS

Making travelling a good experience from the beginning saves problems later and if a good traveller becomes a bad one you must check your trailer, driving style and that the horse has no physical problems making travel uncomfortable.

It is best to sort out loading problems when you are not going anywhere, because it takes time and patience. If you need professional help, common-sense handlers who first form a bond with a horse often get results because trust works better than force.

Get a young or nervous horse used to your trailer by feeding him in there so he associates it with pleasure. If you have twin ramps you

can walk the horse through so he learns that there is a way out, and it may help to follow a good loader or a person he knows.

A common handler fault is to turn and face the stubborn horse, which he may see as a reprimand. You are also obstructing him, so keep facing forwards and encouraging him onwards. Someone in the trailer rattling a feed bucket helps. Once you have him on the trailer, praise him, feed him, then lead him out, remembering he may rush!

As a last resort to get him on (not as normal practice) you need two helpers in hard hats and gloves with two lunge lines. Attach a lunge line to each side of the ramp entrance and ask your helpers to stand so that the lines form a funnel to the ramp. As you lead the horse forwards, the helpers come steadily round behind him, out of kicking range, crossing over and then using the lunge lines pressing against the horse's quarters to encourage him forwards.

Never blindfold a horse or give any more than a firm tap with a schooling whip – bad experiences reinforce distrust. A bridle over the headcollar gives more control.

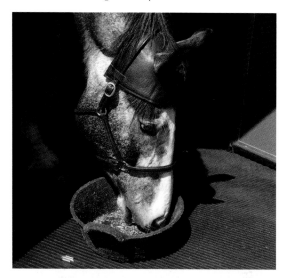

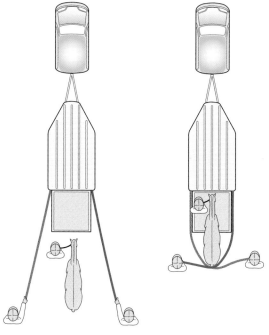

ON THE ROAD

It is essential to give the horse a smooth, safe ride. Good observation enables you to slow down early for hazards, to be in the right gear, position your vehicle correctly and signal early enough to warn others.

Keep an eye on your mirrors so you are not surprised by vehicles overtaking and have a better chance of spotting anyone getting into your blind spots.

Towing speed limits

Urban	Rural single carriageways	Dual-carriageways and motorways
30	**50**	**60**

GEAR CHANGES

Towing accentuates poor gear changes, so unnecessary stress is put on the occupants, car and trailer. When changing up, your throttle foot comes down just after the clutch is fully engaged, but when you change down, the throttle foot starts applying pressure just before the clutch comes up, because a lower gear means higher engine speed.

With modern automatics, learn how and when to use the different shift modes. With off-roaders know how and where to use four-wheel-drive because systems vary and damage is expensive.

CORNERS

Corner slowly to allow the horses to keep their balance – not least because a horse

falling against the side seriously destabilizes the outfit – but try to keep power on so the car pulls the trailer instead of being pushed by it. The trailer follows a tighter cornering line than the towcar, so corner wide and look for cyclists and cars coming up the inside. (Beware of gateposts, too!)

ROUNDABOUTS

Take roundabouts steadily because horses have trouble coping with the repeated direction changes, particularly after dozing on a long, straight stretch. Read *The Highway Code* so you get positioning and signalling right. Get into the correct lane early on your approach.

Beware on roundabouts that other drivers may misjudge their approach to you because they do not appreciate the length of your outfit, your need to drive slowly or your need to turn wide.

RIGHT TURNS

Check your mirrors, signal early and move to a position just left of the road's centre. If someone is following close behind, a hand signal is wise. Stop just short of the centre line of the road you are turning into. If someone is waiting to come out, it is safer to let them go. When safe, turn into the road, aiming close to the nearside kerb to avoid the trailer cutting the corner.

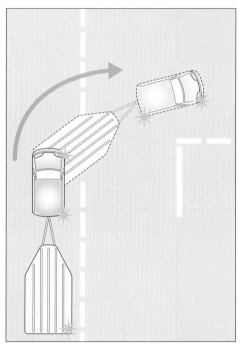

DUAL-CARRIAGEWAYS AND MOTORWAYS

Towcars are not allowed into the right-hand lane of motorways of three or more lanes but are allowed into that lane on three-lane dual-carriageways, though other drivers may not expect it.

Keep checking your mirrors so that the sudden tug of passing lorries and coaches does not surprise you. Do not over-correct when a passing vehicle tugs at yours, just hold it steady.

When changing lanes, signal early and check your blind spot and the closing speed of distant vehicles.

Trailers are affected by side winds, so look for the warnings, like swaying trees and other vehicles wandering. Be careful when emerging from cuttings and when crossing, or going under, bridges.

NARROW ROADS

Take extra care on narrow roads, particularly town streets flanked by parked cars. Oncoming drivers do not always appreciate the amount of space a car and trailer need to pull in and may come on regardless. Using headlights helps draw attention to your vehicle and reduces the risk that others see the car and not the trailer, especially those pulling out of parking spaces.

When you pull out you may have to go to the other side of the road to clear obstacles, so check forwards as well as behind.

ROUGH SURFACES

The picture shows how a wedge that lifts a trailer wheel off the ground does not even tilt the car, so go slowly on bumpy roads and showgrounds because the horse feels bumps more than you do.

SNAKING

It is normal to feel occasional side-to-side movement (yaw) on a trailer, which should have no affect on the towcar, but if it builds up enough to move the towcar it is called snaking and can lead to total loss of control.

A trailer too heavy for the car, a horse losing his balance, cross winds, an overtaking truck, uneven tyre pressures or brakes, swerving and grooves left in the tarmac by lorries' wheels can all trigger snaking. Speed is the overlying factor, which is why you must always be conscious of it and beware of accelerating down hills. Ignore those who suggest trying to accelerate out of a snake – you just have your accident faster!

Come off the throttle smoothly and let the speed drop. Ideally you should not brake, but you may have to if you are going downhill or running out of road, so do it smoothly and gently.

Fighting the yaw by swinging the steering exacerbates it, so keep the steering steady. Easing your grip with one hand may stop your hands 'fighting' each other.

Afterwards, check the car and trailer for any defects responsible for the snaking. If it happens more than once, have the trailer professionally checked and make sure it is not too heavy for your towcar.

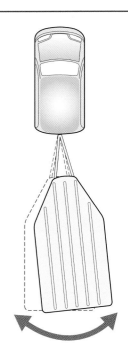

STABILIZERS

A stabilizer is not the answer to an ill-matched outfit but it enhances stability and reduces the risk of snaking. Blade stabilizers like this one also reduce pitching for greater human and animal comfort.

ACCIDENTS AND BREAKDOWNS

⚠️ **DANGER!** Never unload horses on the road or risk them getting out – it is illegal on motorways and has proved fatal. Seek police assistance if you must get horses from a stricken vehicle on a busy road.

Car breakdown organizations will try to fix your towcar at the roadside but none recover trailers with horses aboard. It is wise to join either The Organization of Horsebox and Trailer Owners (01488 657651; www.horsebox-rescue.co.uk) or Equine Rescue Services (01300 348997; www.equinerescue.co.uk). RAC members can add Horse Trailer Assist to their membership for an extra fee (01488 657650; www.rac.co.uk/horse-trailer-assist).

WHAT TO DO ABOUT ACCIDENTS

The Highway Code gives details of the legal requirements if you have an accident.
Use your hazard warning lights and/or warning triangle. Turn off vehicle ignitions, make sure that nobody smokes near damaged vehicles

WHAT TO TAKE

A mobile phone is essential because you can call help without leaving the horses. Have a hands-free kit to use it on the move. You should also have:

- Horse passports • Bridle • Lunge line
- Emergency phone numbers • Breakdown membership card • First aid kits for people and horses • Toolkit • Fire extinguisher • Warning triangle • High-visibility vest • Wheel clamp in case you need to leave the trailer.

Check whether your towcar jack and wheelbrace are suitable for the trailer.
The warning triangle should be placed 50 metres behind your vehicle, further if you are obscured by a bend. *The Highway Code* no longer recommends their use on motorways.

and disconnect the batteries on seriously damaged ones.

Get someone to direct traffic and call the emergency services if necessary. Tend to human casualties before animals, unless the horses are endangering people.

Always keep an eye on traffic – drivers may pay too much attention to the accident to notice people!

WHAT TO DO ABOUT BREAKDOWNS

Try to get your vehicle to a safe place and use the hazard warning lights and/or warning triangle. Check your location before calling your breakdown organization.

Punctures You should be able to change a wheel on the towcar or trailer without unloading the horses, but you must take care that moving horses do not pull the vehicle off the jack. If you decide to unhitch a laden trailer to work on the car, be careful that it cannot tip onto its tail.

Loosen wheelnuts before jacking up. A

wedge jack is safest for the trailer but, with a conventional one, use the axle or substantial part of the chassis as a jacking point, not the floor. Tighten wheelnuts in diagonal pairs and check tightness after 30 miles.

MOTORWAY EMERGENCIES

More fatal accidents happen on the hard shoulder than on the carriageway itself, so use your hazard lights as soon as you stop and get as far to the left as you can without risking sinking in the verge. Get people onto the verge, but keep as far from the traffic as possible.

Take note of the number on the nearest blue and white marker post, which also shows the direction to the nearest emergency phone. You do not need money or to be a breakdown organization member to use the phones, which connect to a Highways Agency control room, getting you to the right people quicker than a mobile. The operator needs to know your problem, location (the marker number helps) and whether you are a breakdown organization member. Give them your mobile number. Tell them you have horses and do not hang up until they tell you to in case they do not have all the information necessary. Tell the police of your presence even if you can handle the problem alone.

To return to the carriageway, pick up speed on the hard shoulder and signal before moving over.

REVERSING

⚠️ **WARNING** Never reverse a trailer without checking behind you because of the huge blind spot. Have someone see you back in busy places.

Reversing a trailer can be mastered with a little perseverance by anyone who has learned the basic theory, so read this section then keep trying until you get it right. It helps to have someone patient who *can* reverse to tell you where you are going wrong. For the test, learn the reversing exercise explained in Photographic Guide 44, *Preparing for the Towing Test.*

STEP-BY-STEP REVERSING

Start learning by reversing to the right because that is easier than going left, when you have to rely more on mirrors. If you are not sure which way your wheels are pointing, lean out and look. It may help to hold the bottom of the steering wheel so your hands move in the trailer's direction.

Many pre-1989 trailers have a lever that disconnects the brakes for reversing.

1. Start with the outfit straight and about a trailer's length from the place you are reversing into. You need plenty of room to swing the towcar round.

2. Watching the trailer out of the driver's window, reverse slowly and start turning the steering to the left. It is easier to add more steering than correct too much.

3. As soon as the trailer starts to turn, you begin straightening up while still reversing. If you leave it too late, the trailer 'jack-knifes' like this, getting to such an acute angle to the towcar that it cannot be manoeuvred in reverse.

4. Eventually you start steering the other way, while still reversing, to bring the towcar's nose round – but

WHY STEER THE 'WRONG WAY'?

Imagining looking down on your reversing outfit may help you to understand why you steer the 'wrong way'. To make the back of the trailer go right, the front must go left. As its front is attached to the back of the car, the back of the car must go left too, so you have to steer left to start the trailer going right. But you only have to steer the 'wrong way' to start the trailer going the opposite way, which is why you begin straightening up as soon it begins turning. Steering can only affect a moving trailer.

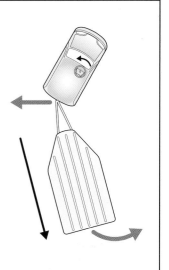

keep an eye on the trailer's direction in case it needs correction.

5. Reverse in a straight line by using the door mirrors: when more of the trailer appears in one mirror, you steer towards that mirror to start the trailer going the other way. This only requires small steering movements.

6. Do not get your mind stuck in reverse! If the trailer goes out of line, it may be easier to pull forward to correct it. On tight turns, or if it jack-knifes, this is the only way.

MAINTENANCE

Trailer care is fully explained in Photographic Guide 26, *Trailer Maintenance*.

CLEANLINESS

Clean out your trailer after each use and allow the floor to dry before shutting it up. A power washer is useful.

Damp bedding encourages floor rot while breeding germs and mould spores, which affect horses' lungs. Caked road dirt promotes corrosion.

Parking on hard standing helps preserve trailer floors by reducing dampness rising from the ground.

TRAILER SERVICING

If you are unable to do it yourself, get the trailer serviced at least annually by a trailer or caravan dealer.

All overrun brake mechanisms have at least one grease nipple which lubricates the sliding part of the system, to which the hitch is attached. Inject grease into these with a grease gun every 2,000 to 3,000 miles. At the same intervals, use white spirit to clean old grease and dirt out of the hitch cup, and check it for wear and damage.

Occasionally oil moving parts on the brake linkage and hitch, plus ramp hinges and locks. Regularly lift the mats to inspect the floor.

Trailers need their drum brakes adjusting every 2,500 to 3,000 miles or at least annually and their wheel bearings greased every two years unless they are a sealed-for-life type. Both are vital maintenance jobs explained in most trailer handbooks.

Check inside lamps annually for corrosion on the bulb holder contacts and give them a protective squirt of WD40.

When necessary, clean the trailer's electrical plug and car socket contacts with a Hella Kleenaplug (from caravan dealers) and spray with WD40.

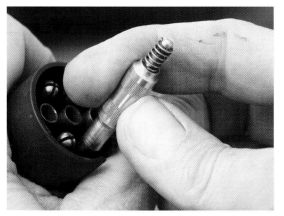

SECURITY

Trailer theft is big business so insurance companies usually insist on a wheel clamp while parked, including at shows. Thieves have dragged away trailers secured with a hitchlock alone, or with a clamp on a front wheel, by hooking the hitch over a pickup tailboard!

Think like a thief when you buy a security device – can it be levered off or cut through easily, is it vulnerable to bolt croppers (most padlocks are) or could you hammer or drill the lock out?

If the trailer has a detachable electrical cable, store it indoors. Keep a note of its chassis number and mark the trailer to show it is yours – perhaps with a rooftop postcode or reflective stripes. Putting your address or postcode in a secret place also helps identify it if stolen.

ACKNOWLEDGEMENTS

Ifor Williams Trailers Ltd., Cynwyd, Corwen, Denbighshire, for the HB505R Classic trailer and advice. Land Rover Ltd., Solihull, West Midlands, for the Range Rover and advice. Leisure Crafts (Bridgnorth) Ltd., Much Wenlock, Salop, for the Bulldog wheelclamp and twin-blade stabilizer. Horseware, Ireland, for the travelling boots and rug worn by Glenn, and Comfort Equestrian for the Transit rug. Equibrand, Charwelton, Northants, for the Coupling Mirror, roof postcodes, Trailer Aid wedge jack and reflective stripe kit. Annie (16.2 hh) Glenn (14.2 hh) and my wife Carolyn (5 ft 6 in) for patient modelling.

First published in Great Britain in 1996
Reprinted 1999, 2000, 2001
This revised edition 2004
Reprinted 2005 (twice), 2006 (twice), 2007, 2008
Reprinted with amendments 2009 and 2010

ISBN 978-0-85131-907-0

J.A. Allen
Clerkenwell House
Clerkenwell Green
London EC1R 0HT

J.A. Allen is an imprint of Robert Hale Limited
www.halebooks.com

A catalogue record for this book is available from the British Library

Photographs by the author
Edited by Martin Diggle
Design and typesetting by Paul Saunders
Line illustrations by Rodney Paull

Colour separation by Tenon & Polert Colour Scanning Limited, Hong Kong
Printed by Gutenberg Press Limited, Malta